The Heart of the Roar

By
Oscar Jones

The Heart of the Roar

By
Oscar Jones

Detroit, MI

The Heart of the Roar

By Oscar Jones

Published by Destiny House Publishing, LLC

Copyright © March 2013 Oscar Jones

ISBN-978-1-936867-81-3

Unless otherwise stated, all scripture quotations are from the Holy Bible, New International Version.

Scripture references that do not have the Bible version noted are the author's paraphrase.

Cover design and Publication Layout: Destiny House Publishing, LLC

Editing: Destiny House Publishing, LLC

ALL RIGHTS RESERVED

All rights reserved under International Copyright law. No part of this book may be reproduced or transmitted in any form or by any means: electronic, mechanical, including photocopying and recording, or by any information storage and retrieval system, without permission in writing from the publisher.

Printed in the United States of America

For information:

Destiny House Publishing, LLC

www.destinyhousepublishing.com

email: inquiry@destinyhousepublishing.com

P.O. Box 19774 Detroit, MI 48219
888-890-9455

Table of Contents

Acknowledgements/Dedications viii

Introduction xi

Chapter 1

The Making of his Mane 1

Chapter 2

Regaining Maturity 13

Chapter 3

The Father's Wound 25

Chapter 4

Presence of His Mane

(Healing the Wounds) 39

Chapter 5

Lovingly Leading Your Family 49

Chapter 6

The Heart of the Roar 61

Chapter 7
The Heart of Champion 73

Acknowledgments/Dedication

I acknowledge Jesus Christ as my King, Ruler, the Leader and Restorer of my own roar. All glory and honor go to him. This journey of manhood is one for an entire lifetime. But, I have learned to celebrate every little victory along the way. So this book is one of those revelatory moments in the journey for me. I have many testimonies which I will share at a later time.

I give thanks to my wife and lioness, Prophetess Crystal Jones, who was my encourager and editor during this process.

I dedicate this book to my sons: Jake Allen, Christopher Jones & Erik Dean
Also, I want to dedicate to the men of Greater Works Family Ministries and those that are a part of Marriage for a Lifetime Ministries.

And finally to my sons in the gospel: Terence Gary, Keith Grier, Damon Harris, Anthony McCray, Adam White, and Randy Winans

Pastor Gregory Colbert, Jeffrey Daniels, Elder Cleaver Davis, Pastor Thomas Hooks, Pastor David Houston, Prophetess James Morris-Stapleton, Pastor Kenneth Nears, Pastor Christopher Willis, and Pastor Tony Winans

x

Introduction

Jesus Christ came to this earth for the specific job of restoring man to God. He has done everything he ever needed to do for this to happen. But like the Israelites, and many Christians before us, there are times when we forget what God has done for us. As men, we turn away from God. We tend to ignore his call on our lives, and forget that being a Christian is a lifestyle, not just a thing we do from time to time.

It's only in Christ, that our roar can be restored. It's only through the power of the Holy Spirit that we can grow in our knowledge of the things of God. And it's only in Christ that we do not lack any thing pertaining to our roar and our families.

Psalm 80 is a prayer to God for restoration:

Hear us, O Shepherd of Israel, you who lead Joseph like a flock; you who sit enthroned between the cherubim, shine forth before Ephraim, Benjamin and Manasseh. Awaken your might; come and save us. Restore us, Oh God; make your face shine upon us, that we may be saved." In verse 7, "Restore us, O God almighty; make your face shine upon us, that we may be saved." And again verse 19, "Restore us, O God almighty; make your face shine upon us, that we may be saved."

Chapter 1

The Making of his Mane

One of the most recognizable characteristics about a lion is its mane. The mane is comprised of long, thick hair that surrounds the head and neck area. The mane gives the lion the appearance of being larger and stronger. This helps the lion in protecting his pride. It also helps protect the lion from injury during fights. Scientists also believe that the coloring of the mane is related to the health of the animal and possibly indicating strong reproductive abilities.

The mane makes the lion look more impressive. It is a very distinct visual signal, which is why we as humans remember it so well. It can be seen from far off. With a mane, the lion looks intimidating. This seems to be the primary function.

It is likely that lions can recognize each other from their manes. It has been said that the darker and fuller the mane, the healthier the lion. The mane of a lion can also be threatening. The lion's mane is thought to make the animal look bigger so it can fight off other animals.

So it is with us as men of God, it is only in the mane of God's presence, that we are able to fight off the spirit of the enemy. We must be willing to fight to stay in his presence.

The lion's mane takes about 3 to 4 years to grow. As the lion grows, the mane becomes fuller. His mane is a source of protection in fighting. It protects his throat area; it keeps another lion from getting to it.

We must mature in worship and in prayer. Just as the mane takes time to develop on the lion, we must take our time and mature in prayer and worship with God. For it is only in that time of worship and prayer that our roar is developed.

So God created man in his *own* image, in the image of God created he him; male and female created he them. 28And God blessed them, and God said unto them, be fruitful, and multiply, and replenish the earth, and subdue it:

and have dominion over the fish of the sea, and over the fowl of the air, and over every living thing that moveth upon the earth. 29And God said, Behold, I have given you every herb bearing seed, which *is* upon the face of all the earth, and every tree, in the which *is* the fruit of a tree yielding seed; to you it shall be for meat. 30And to every beast of the earth, and to every fowl of the air, and to everything that creepeth upon the earth, wherein *there is* life, *I have given* every green herb for meat: and it was so. 31And God saw everything that he had made, and, behold, *it was* very good. And the evening and the morning were the sixth day.

We have dominion over our territory, but our mane must

develop. Mane growth is regulated by the hormone testosterone. Male lions begin growing manes when they are around a year old, and by the time they are four years of age, the mane is fully grown.

A lion's mane may be comprised of anything from dark foot-long tresses to a sparse crop of blond fur framing the neck and face. Manes are variable from one lion to the next, and an individual lion's mane characteristics can also change in response to climactic conditions and other factors.

Some lions are so heavily maned that the long dark fur covers not only their heads and necks but also their foreheads, shoulders, and bellies. In some cases, there are even tufts of fur on the elbows. In other words God has equipped the lion for battle just like He equips us. Our strength and mane development is dependent upon the time we spend with God. Our worship experiences vary.

God has given us the authority and power to rule and lead. So, let's talk about the thing that has hindered many men in the development of their own manes.

The answer lies in the development of our manhood. The mane of the lion is a symbol of maturity. It is an indicator that the lion has grown up.

As we see in the research, lionesses prefer mature males. As a man matures, he is able to deal with matters of the heart.

God has commanded us to act like men. There are four things God has command us to do, in the development of our manhood.

1. Be on the alert.

1 Peter 5:8 Be sober, be vigilant; because your adversary the devil, as a roaring lion, walked about, seeking whom he may devour.

This speaks of being aware of the enemies of your life. Be aware of the battle you're in. It's a spiritual battle, and the devil is trying to lull you and dull you to sleep. Wake up and take your post as a man— as a spiritual leader. Think military. Others depend on you being alert, awake, and aware of enemies trying to steal from you, your family, and your church. The mature lion stands guard over his pride (family). He is at the perimeter of his territory watching for the enemies.

2. Stand firm in the faith.

1 Timothy 6:12 Fight the good fight of faith, lay hold on eternal life, whereunto thou art also called, and hast professed a good profession before many witnesses.

Don't let go of your confidence in God and in His Word. The battle we are in is called "the fight of faith." Life and the devil are trying to push us off our foundation the Word of God. The enemy knows it's the only foundation that can endure all the storms of life. So stand firm in the faith and place your confidence squarely and solely on God's Word and promises.

The alpha male will be tested on a consistent basis. He must defend his territory, it is the same way your faith is going to be tested. Stand firm and believe God.

3. Act like Men.

1 Corinthian 16:13 Watch ye, stand fast in the faith, quit you like men, be strong.
This means to be bold and brave; to have courage. This means never running from our weaknesses, sins or battles; but running to God. Fill your heart up with God's Word to overcome temptation. Whatever is a challenge in your life—attack it, rather than letting it attack you. Be bold enough to say I need help.

Sometime there will be two males defending a territory. In that same way; there are times you will need to be accountable to another. Don't shy away learn to battle together for your pride.

4. Be strong.

Joshua 1: 7-8 Be strong and very courageous. Be careful to obey all the law my servant Moses gave you; do not turn from it to the right or to the left, that you may be successful wherever you go. 8 Do not let this Book of the Law depart from your mouth; meditate on it day and night, so that you may be careful to do everything that is written. This means to be firm, fixed, steadfast—not wishy-washy. Be strong in knowing God's Word. Be strong in consistency. Be strong in knowing how you will respond to situations before they happen.

As lions mature and their manes develop, they become one of the strongest animals in the wild. The maturity has to do more with courage than brutal strength.

The courage of the lion makes him the king of the jungle. There is no fear in his mane. He is able to take down any animal, no matter what the size. It is his belief that he is king that makes him the king.

Chapter 2

Regaining Maturity

We are to be as innocent as lambs in our treatment of others; yet ferocious as LIONS in protecting and advancing our God-given rights and destiny.
As we all know, maturity does not come with age, but with the acceptance of responsibility.

If we are going to grow as men, we have to take full responsibility for our lives; blaming no one. We must own our decisions and decide to grow and change-no matter what comes our way.

In Genesis 3:12, after sinning, Adam said to God, "The woman whom thou hast given to me, she gave me of the tree and I ate.

Adam blamed his wife for his action, a sign of immaturity. Our response to sin in our life will be the measuring stick of our maturity.

We fall for the tricks of the enemy, when we don't really grasp this concept. It's not what we have but who we are.

When we grow in our relationship with God, wisdom is being cultivated. Life brings opportunity to mature. It is in the moments of struggle, pain, rejection, and offense that character can be built. Those things we fear the most are the things God uses to make us.

The lions are very social animals that live in prides. Prides can be composed of up to thirty lions. A lion's family contains one or more males who are often brothers and related adult females and their cubs.

Each pride has its own system of hierarchy. One male dominant lion is looked to as the master of his pride and territory. Living in such close contact requires lions to have very effective communication in order to live together successfully. So within the pride of the lion they realize how important it is to be close.

What is it that sometimes holds men captive in their minds and hearts when it comes to communicating and maturating? There are many reasons, so let's look at a few.

Passivity is one. It has various causes: lack of God's power, lack of hope, negativity, laziness, lack of necessary means.

Think about the way you tend to act when you're about to do something. If there's something that stops you from performing that action, think about the first thought that comes to your mind. Notice the subtle differences between these causes. The more situations you find yourself in, the harder it is for you to do something. God bring these situations to show us the passivity.

God's power gives you the ability to control your thoughts and actions in order to achieve what you want to do; in other words, the ability to <u>go for your dreams</u> and do his will in your family. God is the one that gives us power over that passive spirit, but you must be willing to fight. Get the courage to fight in your mind and spirit. It's already in you. You must draw upon it. So fight.

There is nothing passive about that alpha male, it is his job to protect and govern the pride. He defends the territory from the front; not from behind. If there is going to be an attack the predator is going to have face that alpha male first.

As we read in Genesis 3:1, The woman said to the serpent, "From the fruit of the trees of the garden we may eat; but from the fruit of the tree which is in the middle of the garden, God has said, 'You shall not eat from it or touch it, or you will die". The serpent said to the woman, "You surely will not die! For God knows that in the day you eat from it your eyes will be opened and you will be like God, knowing good and evil". When the woman saw that the tree was good for food, and that it was a delight to the eyes, and that the tree was desirable to make *one* wise, she took from its fruit and ate; and she gave also to her husband with her, and he ate.

Notice, from verse 1 to verse 6, Adam is nowhere to be found. We see the serpent manhandling Eve, with Adam taking a passive role, either just watching or abandoning his post. I really don't know, but he was there.

In order for us to take the lead in our homes, we must mature. We cannot afford to sit passively by and just let life happen. We must rid this spirit from our hearts. To reject passivity, you must hate what it does to you. It leaves you stagnated and unchanged.

Things are the way we allow them to be. So stop tolerating what's not good in your life, and change it.

Matthew 16:19 says God will give you the keys of the kingdom of heaven; whatever you bind on earth will be bound in heaven, and whatever you loose on earth will be loosed in heaven. You have the power to change your circumstances. The beginning of maturity is when we make a decision to not be passive.

Stop doubting yourself. Phil 4:13 says, I can do all things through Christ. We cannot be afraid to fail. God will challenge us to do things we are not comfortable with. We will be put in situations where we must have courage in order to succeed.

Proverbs 29:18 says, 'Where *there is* no vision, the people perish: but he that keepeth the law, happy *is* he.'

Many times men have no vision for their lives. We live for today waiting for something good to happen. And when it doesn't, we see no reason to go the extra mile and we allow passivity to settle in.

What is your defined purpose? As men we must see a reason to act. If we don't, we will allow situations to determine who we are. We will allow passive behaviors to become our lot.

What has God called you to do? Why are you on the earth? Why are you here at this moment in time? I can guarantee you –it's not just for you to go with the flow.

The alpha male attacks any intruder that comes near his pride. He actively goes after the enemy. We must decide to actively go after the devil who comes to steal, kill and destroy you and those around you.

James 4:7. So, let's purposely attack the enemy of passivity in our lives.

First, let's deal with it in our minds. Let's take every thought captive and bring it subject to Christ. Let us not be passive in our worship. Praise, celebration and vulnerability toward God is not just not for women, but us as well. We must go after God with all we have in worship. Worship allows us to see God in a different light. We must go to God and realize we can't do anything without him.

Worship must be our daily bread, if we are going to mature into God's men. Dealing with passivity is a daily assignment. We must be on the lookout. The scripture reminds us, "Woe unto him that is at ease in Zion…" Let us seek God on a daily basis.

Maturity will be evident to our wives and those around us. It is a growing process and takes time. It involves our conscious effort, sacrifice, discipline and grace to say no to whatever God says no to and to say yes when God says yes.

As we overcome passivity we will began to see signs of our growth.

Signs that we have overcome include <u>accepting responsibility for our own actions</u>. This is a big one because we will stop the blame game.

Another sign is an <u>humble spirit</u>. We have to really work on assaulting that spirit of pride in our hearts. A maturing person will be able to recognize pride for what it is. And he will work at killing it in his own life. He may find himself failing in some of his efforts but he won't stay there. He keeps moving forward.

Our goal is to please God and rule our territory. God has given us much and we must properly steward what he has given. The road to success involves willingness on our part and complete trust in God. This is our passion and our life.

Chapter 3

The Father's Wound

Male adult lions are usually only with their prides for 2 to 3 years. They are usually ousted by nomadic lions whose intent is to kill the cubs. Lions do not take kindly to being stepfathers. So most often male lions do not grow up with their fathers.

Even in our society, men do not always remain around to raise their children. Some are incarcerated, some join up with another pride, and others remain, but are emotionally absent. When men are unable to connect with their fathers, a gaping hole is created. This is called the Father's Wound.

The Father's Wound is the absence of love from a birth father. It is the holes created from that absence. There are many wounds that can be created. For some of us this may be a new revelation. However, do not discount the affect of an absent father. It is huge and damaging if not properly dealt with.

I grew up without my father. As a matter of fact I didn't meet my father until I was in my mid forties. As a child, I often wondered about my father. I didn't really seek after an answer but it was a lingering feeling of loss as a child. And it greatly impacted by masculine development.

I was raised by my grandparents. Many times I wondered if there was something wrong with me because I didn't grow up with a father or a mother. It is an unspoken pain many of us live with all our lives. It doesn't go away as you age. The wound goes down deep into the inner chamber of our hearts.

It is in those secret chambers of our hearts that behaviors are formed. This is where secrets are birth, insecurities arise and how we deal with life in general. The father's wound is buried deep in the hearts of men. As a result, we never truly understand our own manhood.

When fathers are absent, physically or emotionally, the wound that results is profound. It touches a man to his core and forever leaves him with the question, *"Am I good enough as a person and a man?"* Every man wants to hear, *"This is my beloved son, in whom I am well pleased."* The truth is that too many men and young males did not and do not hear it enough.

Even if a father was physically present but not emotionally, he still was absent. He was uninvolved in the life of his child, which is perceived by that child, as rejection. That child was left unprotected just as Eve was left vulnerable to the words of the enemy because Adam refused to show up.

In turn, that child turns around and rejects his father. In doing this he shoots himself in the heart. And everywhere he goes for years, he finds himself still searching for the love he never found from his father.

God has given us ability to rule but we can't do it properly, because of this devastating wound. **His mane can't grow out because of the pain of rejection.** In other words, it's going to be harder to reach maturity.

The pain of an absent father goes deep. There is no map or guide.

As a child, I had no one to play catch with, so I often played by myself. Nearly every game I played as a child, I played alone.

When rejection is present and there is no spiritual buffer that child often suffers from a state of isolation. That is the reality of the heart of a child when the father is absent, loneliness.

It is in that loneliness, that Satan uses to bring other vices into life of a lonely hearted child. That child learns to fend for himself and protect himself by any means necessary.

Just as the alpha male protects his pride from outside intruders, so we learn to protect ourselves from outside forces, the best way we can. We learn behaviors that may not be right if we have no one there to teach us.

I thank God for my grandfather. He did the best he could, but he didn't have much left when I came along. He already given himself to his own 14 children, so he had no energy left to parent me.

I eventually found healing in the Chief Physician. I begin to accept

God as my Father. There I found acceptance and love.

It is unfortunate that there are so many men that are raised by single moms. As well meaning as single moms may be, we can only get so much from her. It is the father that must bring that missing piece to our hearts. And in his absence, we learn to protect ourselves through lies, manipulations, and cons to get our way. . Sometimes when these things don't work out, we learn to use violence to try to get our way. Our manhood is being developed haphazardly by trial and error. The reality is ***men need other strong men in their lives.***

Some of us carry the wounds of having been subjected to controlling, manipulative fathers. He was in your life but he wanted to control everything. So you grew up trying to please him and he was never satisfied. Some of you have even chosen careers that weren't your area of passion; but you chose it just to please him.

This type of wound attacks your identity. You have to find significance. It is in who you are in Christ. It is important that we as men find our God given purpose. God created you with a designated purpose. The Father's Wound can keep you from purpose. It will cause you to suffer from low self worth as a result and commonly question your own decisions. You may find it hard to do things on your own.

This wound can get so severe that it will create an approval addiction. This addiction will paralyze you when it's time to make a decision. You are given to lean on the opinions of your father and if he doesn't approve of it, you just won't do it. Sometimes even in church, a man may think that because I am a pastor's son, I am supposed to be a pastor when I get older. Don't get me wrong, God does call some pastor's sons or daughters to the office; but it must be a call of God.

The wound of approval will hinder you in your development. Also you may feel guilty if you don't reach your father's level of expectation. Satan uses guilt to lure you into situations that will be damaging to your manhood. It may be a relationship or a job situation.

You are God's man created in his image allow him to guide you in the direction you should go.

Many of the father wounds we carry come in the form of deceptions from the past. We found out things that hurt us. Perhaps there were things that have been withheld from you, which you subsequently found out, which altered the whole father image you carried.

Father's wounds like these can cause a real crisis of confidence. Their sons ask, "If he can do that, who am I?" Many times we discover breaches in our past. As a result it creates that hole of mistrust.

Also, there is a temptation of blaming our fathers for the

mistakes that we ourselves make. Firstly you need to know that forgiveness not blame is the route to healing. Secondly you need to be aware that God does not hold our fathers accountable for our sins. In Ezekiel 18:4 says, "Every living soul belongs to me, the father as well as the son--both alike belong to me. The soul who sins is the one who will die."

First we must recognize the wound for what it is. We all have sinned and fallen short of the Glory of God. So as fathers we all will fail during our parenting season. So we must have enough grace to extend to our dads. The grace we give to them will heal our own hearts. Because through that grace we see our failure and God's love for us.

Jesus came in order that our dislocation from father God would be set straight. At his baptism in Matthew 3:17 Jesus hears what our hearts are desperate to hear, "This is my son, whom I love with whom I am well pleased".

To those of you who find yourself in the valley of the shadow of death. To those of you who find yourself in a place of desperate need, longing for the fulfillment of your promises…come and ride with Me. Bury your face in the Mane of My Presence and be not afraid. You must praise Me and as you praise Me, I will "ROAR".

Isaiah 31:4

This is what GOD told me. Like a lion, king of the beasts, that gnaws and chews and worries its prey not fazed in the least bit by a bunch of shepherds who arrive to chase it off, So GOD-of-the-Angel-Armies comes down to fight on Mount Zion, to make war from its heights. And like a huge eagle hovering in the sky, GOD-of-the-Angel-Armies protects Jerusalem. I'll protect and rescue it. Yes, I'll hover and deliver."

Know that as you are with the Lord, praising Him he ROARS over your life, where no foe can come near.

 Many young men are growing up without a father who can affirm their leap into manhood. Often the voices they do hear are distortions of true manhood. Their transition is often filled with feelings of fear, anger and frustration, instead of confidence and security. Lonely and discouraged, boys become isolated and alienated men. In this isolated state, men continue to desire closeness and connection, but they often have no concept of how to achieve it.

So as we can see, there have been many things that have hindered the development of our mane. But it is vital that our mane develops if we are to effectively lead our pride.

Chapter 4

The Presence of His Mane
(Healing the Father's Wound)

The Father's wound desperately needs to be healed. Only a father can affirm a man's masculinity and make him feel that he's a man. Neither fame nor fortune nor all the women in the world can ever do this for him. Only a father's love can feed that longing.

But in order for healing to occur, First, we need to acknowledge the fact that we had or have a father's wound that needs healing. As long as we deny this, we can never be healed. If we are hurting, we simply have to admit it.

Many men have been taught that it is weakness to admit you have a problem. So we live in a masculine facade, acting as if all is well. But, it is evident in our relationships, marriages and our children that all is not well. It is imperative that we admit that there is a need.

Secondly, we must forgive. You have heard it said, unforgiveness is like drinking poison hoping the other person dies. **Mark 11:25** says but when you are praying, first forgive anyone you are holding a grudge against, so that you're Father in heaven will forgive your sins, too.

Forgiveness is always in a person's best interest. On the other hand, unforgiveness is toxic. Unforgiveness and bitterness produce stress. Stress is the villain for a plethora of diseases, including hypertension, ulcers, cancer, diabetes, stroke, and many others. So there is a definite need to forgive. But how does one actually walk through the process of forgiveness?

Acknowledge that you were violated. Forgiveness does not require that we **pretend** that the transgression did not occur. Otherwise there is no need to forgive. Forgiveness says, there was indeed an infraction however no payment will be required. Jesus already paid the price.

The decision must be made to forgive. Even though the victim will not immediately "feel" like he has forgiven. He must hold to his decision. Do not meditate on the offense. When thoughts of the wound come up in your mind, think on something positive. Think good thoughts of your father, if possible. If not, speak it out loud, "I choose to forgive." Say it, every time the thought occurs and pray for your offender.

Understand that most times, the father's wound is generational. Your father's father brought him harm and disappointment and his father and so on. So look at your dad with sympathetic eyes. He has or had some broken places in his own life that needed healing. He couldn't give you what he didn't have. So don't hold it against him. Most times, he did not mean to harm you. But even if he did intend to bring harm, that is proof that he is unhealthy and in need of wholeness and deliverance.

Give yourself time. It is not healthy to rush the process. If the wound is deep, the healing will need to go deep. It will take a while before a person will actually "feel" like he has forgiven. Keep working towards it. The benefits outweigh the drawbacks. Not only are you protecting your physical health, but you reap emotional and spiritual advantages, as well. So go ahead, forgive. It's a gift you give yourself.

Colossians 3:13 You must make allowance for each other's faults and forgive the person who offends you. Remember the Lord forgave you, so you must forgive others. Without forgiveness, one remains a prisoner of his past.

Also understand that a man cannot harbor resentment toward his father and have healthy male relationships. One of the main reasons men have problems with relationship with other men is because of the Father's wound. When there is resentment still there, you can't grow. In addition, unresolved anger with a father increases the likelihood of repeating his weaknesses. In other words you are likely to tread down the same path. That is the way a generational curse works. So we must forgive to reverse the curse.

Thirdly, we need to continue to build healthy relationships with other healthy men. Join the men's group in your church, Create relationships with other men. They can aid in your process.

The alpha male lions run together. After lions reach a certain age, they are no longer trained by the lioness. They are affirmed by other male lions and bonding takes place. As you allow bonding to take place with other mature males, it causes you to mature faster. No woman could ever affirm your masculinity enough or teach you to love yourself as a man.

Only men can meet an unmet father's need. As long as a man depends on a woman to make him feel good about himself, he will be emotionally tied to his mother's apron strings. All a woman can ever do is confirm what a man already feels about himself. That is, if he rejects himself as a man, he will likely be attracted to a rejecting woman. Or if he loves and accepts himself as a man, be will be attracted to a loving and accepting woman who will confirm what he feels about himself.

Fourthly, every man needs accountability. He needs to be affirmed by men who become father substitutes. He needs to find men he can trust and let them know him as he truly is - warts and all. Every one of us has a dark side. We need to take the risk and share our dark side to other men we trust; men who will know us fully and accept me as we are. It is through their love and acceptance that we learn to love and accept ourselves. But as long as I keep my dark side hidden, I will never feel fully loved. I can only be loved and healed to the degree that I am known.

Finally, the bottom line to feeling fully loved is to feel God the Father's love at the very core of our being. Herein lies the deepest healing of the masculine soul. Our healing from the Father's wound begins as we see beyond our earthly father to our heavenly father who as it says in Romans 8:23 is adopting us as sons, through the work of his Son, Jesus. When Jesus teaches us to pray in Matthew 6:9 he says begin with 'Our Father'.

I want to tell you that despite the depths of your earthly father's wounds, you are not defined by it. Our Father God is our source. Rely on his love and total acceptance of you. Understanding the fact that the Father accepts you just the way you are is the beginning of the healing process. Your relationship with Christ is essential. We must seek to get in the presence of His mane to be healed. As we are in his presence our mane is developing. You then can learn to feel closer to God and accept his love, just as it is.

It is in His presence where your mane will grow. He is ready to manifest Himself to you. As you run towards your Father's love. Your Father will "celebrate" you and draw you into His amazing grace. Yes, He fully loves you right where you are. God is good all the time.

Chapter 5

Lovingly Leading Your Family

An army of a sheep led by a lion will always defeat an army of lions led by a sheep. -Dr. Myles Munroe

The only way to be manly is to first be Godly. Manliness and Godliness are synonymous.

The male lion leads his pride. He sits at the gate of his territory and secures his pride. His roar is a constant reminder of who is in charge.

God has chosen man to lead his home. The ultimate test of your manhood is not what you do on a field or court, or what you claim you did back in the day. The ultimate test of your leadership is not your ability to launch a business, grow a ministry, develop a team, or contribute to the bottom line. The ultimate test of your manhood and your leadership is your home life. Can you, by God's grace and through His power, help your family become more like Jesus? Can you lead your home? This is a humbling reality for us as men, but God holds us accountable for the spiritual health of our spouses and families.

There are many reasons why men fail to lead; let us look at some. Many times men did not see good male leadership modeled in their own homes as they grew up.

Some men weren't properly instructed by their pastors in their leadership roles as husbands. Men have to be taught how to lead.

Some men are just lazy and would rather relinquish the leadership role in the home to their wives. We see this a lot. Wives sometimes take his role while the husband secretly resents it. However he won't step up to the role himself. These men simply give up when their wives challenge them for the leadership of the home as their wives remind them of all their poor decisions in the past. Also, in some extreme cases, husbands are manipulated by their wives through tears, denial of sex, or constant verbal harassment to relinquish leadership.

It is man's God-ordained responsibility to take responsibility as the leader of the home. It is essential to understand that none of these reasons are valid excuses that God would ever accept for a husband not being the leader of his home.

So let's look at how we should lead:

1. Loving Leading your home

A husband's leadership role in the home must first be firmly rooted in love. Love is the core principle that should govern everything you say and do. Ephesians 5:25 Husband love your wife like Christ love is for the Church. Jesus is your ultimate example of a leader. He was strong and yet tender as the circumstances required. He knew when to be the lion and when to be the lamb. He could drive the money changers out of the Temple, but hold a child in His arms or weep over Jerusalem. Therefore, let all that you do as a husband and a leader in your home be done with strength, honor, boldness, and with the tenderness of love.

2. Leading by initiating.

Most of us wait on our wives to do everything. Leading requires initiating. The coach doesn't wait for the players to come up with plays.

If you love your wife as Christ loved the church, you will become an initiator in your relationship. You will initiate the spiritual tone in your home. You will initiate prayer and family devotions. You will be the initiator in problem solving and communication to deal with conflicts or how money is to be spent. You will initiate opportunities to spend time with your spouse. You will take the lead in these and other areas of your marriage because you are the leader.

As you do, your wife will come to realize, in a very practical way, how much you care about her and the well-being of your family. Your leadership will cause her to trust you.

3. Leading by example.

Being an example is especially important if you desire your wife and children to have a sincere respect for you as the leader of your home. Do you want your wife and children to simply respect you because you are the head of your home, or because they see your godly behavior, loving actions, and walk of faith? As men, respect is a primary need. Your lifestyle before your wife and children will determine your level of respect.

4. Leading in reconciliation

A godly man does not hold grudges. Is this the way you deal with the conflicts with your wife and children? Are you the one who takes the lead and steps forward first? Do you admit your fault and seek resolution or turn and walk away? Aren't you glad Jesus took the leadership in your life to come and seek reconciliation with you? Begin to take the leadership in this area of your home. Forgive quickly.

God has entrusted us with a great responsibility.

We are responsible for the pride God has entrusted to us. How do we lead? All headship must be done by love as I stated earlier. **Husbands, love your wives, just as Christ loved the church and gave himself up for her."** Did Jesus come demanding blind obedience just because He said so? Not at all! He did not come demanding to be served. Rather, He came to serve and to love.

If your wife is submitting to you but you are not submitting to Christ as His servant, then your wife is being obedient to Him but you are not. You were never meant to be your wife's master. You were meant to be her spiritual leader. And if she is obeying Christ by following you but you are not obeying Him by following Him, you can leave your wife bitter and resentful towards you and towards God.

We are to loving lead our children as well **Col. 3:21** says Fathers are not to provoke their children to wrath. "Provoke" carries the idea of inciting them to anger or resentment, making them bitter, disturbing or troubling their minds. This leads to discouragement. "Discouraged means to be disheartened, dispirited and broken in spirit".

Other parental responsibilities include: teaching (Dt. 6:7, 20-22)

⁷And thou shalt teach them diligently unto thy children, and shalt talk of them when thou sittest in thine house, and when thou walkest by the way, and when thou lies down, and when thou risest up, to train. Our charge as a leader is to lead them in family devotions and train them in scripture as they grow.

(Prov. 22:6) Train up a child in the way he should go: and when he is old, he will not depart from it. Isaiah 38:19 The living, the living, he shall praise thee, as I do this day: the father to the children shall make known thy truth.

(Eph. 6:4), Fathers, do not provoke your children to anger by the way you treat them. Rather, bring them up with the discipline and instruction that comes from the Lord.

(1 Tim. 3:4), He must manage his own family well and see that his children obey him with proper respect.

We must be willing to do the hard things, the things that may make us uncomfortable. It is easy to lead our way which may mean a variance of way. But true leadership must be selfless. A selfless leader will always put the need of his pride first.

Jesus gave all of himself in love. As husbands we are to give of ourselves in love.

Heart of the Roar is to lead no matter what and who may come against you. To lead is an amazing thing. Your headship will always be undermined by Satan. He hates leadership. In order to move forward headship must be in place. So the enemy works to keep men out of our places. The lion realizes he must guard the perimeter of the territory he has, because if he doesn't he could lose everything.

We are in a war for headship of our home. Either we will lead or we will relinquish it over to the devil. Lead with the authority Christ has given you and you will see God's glory revealed in your family.

Chapter 6

The Heart of the Roar

Be strong and of a good courage for unto this people shalt thou divide for an inheritance the land, which I sware unto their fathers to give them. Only be thou strong and very courageous, that thou mayest observe to do according to all the law, which Moses my servant commanded thee: turn not from it *to* the right hand or *to* the left, that thou mayest prosper whithersoever thou goest. This book of the law shall not depart out of thy mouth; but thou shalt meditate therein day and night, that thou mayest observe to do according to all that is written therein: for then thou shalt make thy way prosperous, and then thou shalt have good success. Have not I commanded thee? : Be strong and of a good courage; be not afraid, neither be thou dismayed: for the LORD thy God *is* with thee whithersoever thou goest. Joshua 1:6-8. God told Joshua to be strong and courageous.

Interesting that the lion isn't the biggest nor the strongest animal in the animal kingdom, yet he is called the king of the beasts. One of the main reasons is that the lion is labeled with that title is because of his courage. Courage is the ability to conquer fear or despair: and have bravery and valor in the time of need. There is no fear in the heart of a lion.

Each of us has been given that type of heart whether we know it or not. For God has not given us the spirit of fear, but power, love and a sound mind. We have the mind of Christ.

We all know the story of the Cowardly Lion in the classic movie "The Wizard of Oz" he overcame all kinds of threats and obstacles (with Dorothy, the Tin Man, and the Scarecrow) to get to the Wizard, who gave him his courage in the form of a medal. Turns out, he already had it – he just didn't believe it. After all, he was a lion, leader of the pack. He is the king of the Savanna. He really didn't have to go through all that trouble to prove himself.

But why didn't he believe in who he was? He didn't understand the power he possessed. The spirit of fear grips the heart of men. There are many reasons why this happens. We have discussed many of them already in this book. Just as the lion was taken from his mother as a cub, many of us are raised without proper parental guides. And because of that we don't know we are a king. So, the lion didn't know that he was a king. He didn't know that he was a magnificent animal and was a symbol of power and courage.

We also don't fully comprehend that we are fearfully and wonderfully made. We are made in His image. In fact, the Bible says that we are made to God kings and priests. (Revelation 1:6)

When a man of God doesn't know who he is and whose he is, he never acquires the necessary lessons of life to <u>warrant</u> him to reign as king. We must do the things required to become the men of God He created us to be. If we lack necessary tools, we cannot settle for who the world says that we are.

We must follow the pattern of who God says that we are.

The world says men don't show emotions, so we learn to bottle up our true feelings. The world says men don't cry, so we learn how to deal with pain without relief. So a worldly man essentially withers to become nothing more than a wimpy kitten. This man who has been stripped of his courage and his identity allows life to pass him by with regret after regret.

Through his journey with Dorothy, the cowardly lion was forced to step into the role he was meant to live and found that his courage was always there.

So it is when men find their roar. What makes the difference? He was loved and developed love for his companions. He had a reason to dig deep enough to find that courage, confidence and power within. The cowardly lion found a reason, to look within.

When we find Jesus and allow Him to take us on this journey to discover our manhood, our lives will change. The lion in the Oz story was loved. When we recognized we are loved, this is our key. We must know and accept that we are loved by the Father. Through that love you can began to see who you are in Christ and who He is in you. The fictional lion didn't know how strong he was until being strong was the only choice he had. Sometimes God allows situations in our lives to show us what's in us.

The cowardly lion discovered his strength when he was put into a situation. Men, we are strong. When we allow Christ to work through us, it's not of our own strength but it's His. The lion is strong and he recognizes it. You must see yourself as strong. The Word says let the weak say I am strong.

Courage is required in almost every basic human activity or endeavor. For instance, to allow yourself to love and commit to another person takes immense courage.

Lions are very social creatures; they are committed to their pride. The courage it takes for them to roam and protect each day is great.

We, too, are social creatures and it does take courage for men to open up to other men and women, as well. We must learn to love beyond ourselves as we grow. It takes courage and power to commit for life in our relationships.

To survive an abusive, traumatic or abandoned childhood with some sense of dignity and integrity intact demonstrates tremendous courage and resilience.

For most of us, growing older demands courage. To persevere rather than to quit. To act with integrity rather than being a crowd pleaser. To take responsibility rather than put blame. To embrace reality rather than retreat from it. To move forward in life rather than regress or stagnate. To create rather than destroy. To love rather than hate. To deal with your own imperfections, rather than not. To consciously face the inevitable facts of life rather than denying them.

Courage is living out the Word without compromise.

Like the Cowardly Lion, who constantly looks for courage

outside himself, we may already be more courageous, more heroic, than we've imagined.

He was called Cowardly because of his past. But that was not who he was. God doesn't call us by our past. He calls us by our future. He called Abraham a man of faith. He called Gideon a mighty man of Valor.

Let's move on to acknowledging our past acts of courage, tapping into our innate capacity to be courageous. And move forward in demonstrating courage even in the presence of our weaknesses.

Courageous people know what they must do and they do it, even though they may be very much afraid.

The lesson here is that courage isn't about acting in the absence of fear. It's about acting regardless of our fears. Knowing who you are and whose you are! Ask yourself this, 'If God before me, who and what can be against me? For the Lion of Judah goes before you!!! *Psalm 8:31*.

The truth is you have the Heart of the Roar already on the inside.

Chapter 7

Heart of a Champion

Champions are not those who never fail, but those who never quit. ~Edwin Louis Cole.

Champions are men in whom courage has become visible. The site of the Alpha male strikes fear in the heart of most animals. They recognize that the lion is fearless. So, they give reverence to the champion of the jungle. We also are champions in the spirit. God created us to be champions. Therefore in the heart of every man is a champion spirit.

David was a champion. In 1 Samuel 17:4 A champion named Goliath, who was from Gath, came out of the Philistine camp. His height was six cubits and a span. . This worldly champion can out to fight against Israel. They were afraid because they couldn't recognize themselves as champions. Nearly the entire army stood trembling in fear as Goliath assailed his threats.

The trick of the devil to keep us from understanding who we are in Christ. And for some reason, this trick was working on Israel. We as men of God need not ever fear. 1 John 4:4 Ye are of God, little children, and have overcome them: because greater is he that is in you, than he that is in the world.

It is God that works in you the things He wants worked through you. In other words, God will prepare you for the battles of life.

Being a champion has nothing to do with you, and everything to do with Jesus.

In 1 Samuel we see as well God's Champion. 1 Samuel 17: 45 David said to the Philistine, "You come against me with sword and spear and javelin, but I come against you in the name of the Lord Almighty, the God of the armies of Israel, whom you have defied. 46 This day the Lord will deliver you into my hands, and I'll strike you down and cut off your head. This very day I will give the carcasses of the Philistine army to the birds and the wild animals, and the whole world will know that there is a God in Israel. 47 All those gathered here will know that it is not by sword or spear that the Lord saves; for the battle is the Lord's, and he will give all of you into our hands.

You see guys it not by our power or might that we are champions, it is by His power. We cannot believe we can do anything in our own strength. But just as the boy David says, we come against the enemy in the name of the Lord.

Too often as men we try to rely on our own strength. This interferes with the development of our faith. We must avoid self sufficiency. It will keep us locked in unbelief. If we believe that we have to do everything on our own, we will have a defeatist attitude. Some things we won't even try. Let me tell you about the boy David. He had gained faith experience prior to this encounter with Goliath. He had defeated a lion and a bear while tending the sheep. So He knew what God was capable of. He understood that there was no earthly strength to match that of the God he served.

2Corinthian 3:5 Not that we are sufficient of ourselves to think anything as of ourselves; but our sufficiency is of God.

We have to careful when you get any type of success. God is our source of success period. When we take credit for ourselves, we lose. We fork over victories to the enemy.

We could say that the theme song of every believing male is 'We Are The Champions'. It is our call, our mandate. You were created to be competitive, to dominate, and to rule. It is part of our nature. The aggressive spirit of a man is purposed by God. But, we must allow the Spirit of God to tame that part of our nature. Notice, I said tame, not take it away.

We cannot think that aggression is ungodly. We must be aggressive against our enemy. We must use all our power and might to take him down. But the heart of the champion is tamed by the Holy Spirit. And he never turns that aggression on his pride. He is surrendered to the Spirit of Christ. So a champion doesn't abuse his wife or children verbally, physically or emotionally.

A champion is able to face his own failures. The way we view failure will determine how far we will go. I know for most of us, we would rather cut off a right arm than fail.

Sometimes it's that very failure that God uses to bring out the champion spirit that is already in our hearts.

You see I failed miserly as a husband. Now I could give you tons of excuses trying to justify myself but the bottom line is I failed. But it was in those failures that God ministered to me and used those instances to bring out the champion that I was to become today. God healed my marriage and gave me the awesome privilege of being a champion to my wife. I learned and I am still learning to love her like Christ's loves His bride. I did not sit down and roll over in my failure. I got up and took it to the Lord.

Every man will experience some type of failure in his life. The question is what will he do with it? He may lose a home, his business, a job, investments, a child to sickness or drugs. He may lose his marriage or a position. How does a champion respond to trouble that may have been his fault?

Watch ye, stand fast in the faith, quit you like men, be strong. 1 Corinthians 16:13. Stand fast in faith. Guys we may fail, but we have a God of a second chance. He will be with us, bringing out the champion in us at every opportunity. He is a merciful, loving, compassionate God. He showers us when we are honest with him. His love covers. Champions practice in private to succeed in public. Earlier I talked about worship as it relate to us. I am a firm believer that we are as strong as our worship. In other words, the more you worship the stronger you become in spirit. It is in those private moments of worship that we really see God for who he really is. It is in those times that God can really speak to our heart and infuse us with the power of the roar.

The tendency is that we love the accolades of succeeding without giving up ourselves. So we look for shortcuts or we try to ride on the back of someone else's success story. But, God wants to give you your own story. Each man should have his own story of success so others can see and be encouraged.

Intrinsic to every success story is the conflict, the malfunction, the collapse. Something didn't work or work out. Something went wrong. You see, there must be a need for a champion. The rescuer has to have someone who needs rescuing. You can never be a champion standing outside of the ring. You will never be a champion if you easily give up. A champion stands toe to toe, flat-footed against the enemy of his soul. He fights for his marriage, even if his wife won't fight. He fights for his children, when they have given up. He is not the loser who just walks away with his head held down.

That alpha male knows if he is not the champion for his pride, he will not have them long. So he gives himself up so that he can be the champion to those cubs and lioness in his pride. He risks it all for them. Sometimes he fails at taking down the prey. Sometimes he doesn't win the battle. But he is always ready for the fight.

Be your wife and children's earthly champion. They need a champion in their lives. Be that champion that would give all for those he loves the most.

Being a champion isn't an option for the Alpha male and neither is it for us. Jesus is a champion for the church, his bride. He is the rescuer. In that same way, we must be for our bride. Allow God to bring out the champion in you, it's there. Because in the heart of a champion is the Heart of the roar.

David took down an enemy that was physically bigger and stronger than himself. Goliath was actually no match for little David. Because

David was strong in His faith. He was sure of His God. Men, we are champions in God's kingdom. We simply must believe God is who He says He is. Let's live like we are champions in our homes, in our communities, of the world. .

BIO of Oscar Jones

Pastor Oscar was born and raised in Mississippi. After he graduated from high school, he moved on to Jackson State University where he met and married his college sweetheart, Prophetess Crystal Jones. He & his bride have been celebrating their covenant love for more than 32 years. Their passion for one another has yielded a fruitful harvest of 5 adult children, 2 bonus children (in-laws) and 6 delightful grandchildren.

The two have a unique team ministry. They lavishly love the Lord and one another. God has coupled this into a special anointing and gifted them to be able to minister from the pulpit as one voice.

Apostle Oscar and his one flesh partner, pastor **Greater Works Family Ministries** in Detroit, MI and are founders of **Marriage For A Lifetime Ministries, and are apostolic overseers of Agape International Association of Churches and Para-churches** (a ministry to pastors and leaders).

Oscar is a trailblazer with a strong deliverance ministry. He has a fervor for men's ministry; teaching men the principles of authentic manhood. He is zealous about the word of God. And believes in living the gospel that he preaches.

Oscar hosts a Restore the Roar's Men's Conference and Rally. He has hosted both events all across the country.

Oscar also has an international call on his life. He has ministered in Rota, Spain and Coimbatore, India.

The heartbeat of his call is to repair the breaches. He and his wife are dedicated to offering healing and hope to marriages and families. Oscar has ministered at workshops, retreats, conferences and other special events all across the country; breaking denominational barriers. He and his wife have been featured guests on several radio and television broadcasts. He has also authored and co-authored many books with the love of his life.

Contact Oscar Jones
Marriage For A Lifetime
Ministries
P.O. Box 19774
Detroit, MI 48219
www.marriage4alifetime.org
jones@marriage4alifetime.org
206.600.5728

Books By The Author

Extreme Money Makeover by Oscar & Crystal Jones

LeaderShift 3.0 by Oscar & Crystal Jones

Naked Sex (For Married Couples Only) by Oscar & Crystal Jones

Restore The Roar by Oscar Jones

Ring Talks by Oscar & Crystal Jones

The Newlywed Handbook by Oscar & Crystal Jones

When The Vow Breaks by Oscar & Crystal Jones

www.ingramcontent.com/pod-product-compliance
Lightning Source LLC
Chambersburg PA
CBHW060846050426
42453CB00008B/859